THE HISTORY

OF POLAND

A Fascinating Guide to this European Country

Andrew Green

© **Copyright 2020 - All rights reserved.**

The content contained within this book may not be reproduced, duplicated or transmitted without direct written permission from the author or the publisher.

Under no circumstances will any blame or legal responsibility be held against the publisher, or author, for any damages, reparation, or monetary loss due to the information contained within this book, either directly or indirectly.

Legal Notice:

This book is copyright protected. It is only for personal use. You cannot amend, distribute, sell, use, quote or paraphrase any part, or the content within this book, without the consent of the author or publisher.

Disclaimer Notice:

Please note the information contained within this document is for educational and entertainment purposes only. All effort has been executed to present accurate, up to date, reliable, complete information. No warranties of any kind are declared or implied. Readers acknowledge that the author is not engaging in the rendering of legal, financial, medical or professional advice. The content within this book has been derived from various sources. Please consult a licensed professional before attempting any techniques outlined in this book.

By reading this document, the reader agrees that under no circumstances is the author responsible for any losses, direct or indirect, that are incurred as a result of the use of information contained within this document, including, but not limited to, errors, omissions, or inaccuracies.

TABLE OF CONTENTS

INTRODUCTION 1

THE FIRST DAYS OF POLAND 6

THE END OF THE MIDDLE AGES IN POLAND 11

THE EARLY MODERN HISTORY OF POLAND...................... 17

THE MODERN HISTORY OF POLAND 24

THE ECONOMY OF POLAND 34

THE DEMOGRAPHICS OF POLAND 40

THE POLITICS OF POLAND 45

THE GEOGRAPHY OF POLAND 54

CONCLUSION 60

INTRODUCTION

When comparing the histories of countries, there are time periods in every country that can exist as a blight on the country's historical record. These blights can vary in size and can exist for a myriad of reasons; however, as is true with most types of leadership, the source of these blights can often be traced to the radical or unethical beliefs of a singular individual. Every country has its own blight, and it is the responsibility of the citizens to rise above that blight, showing the world that the actions of one man in one point of history do not dictate the ethics or success of the country. One such country that has endured a particularly terrible blight is Poland. While Poland is a beautiful country nestled in the heart of Europe, there is hardly an individual who can think of Poland without thinking of the atrocities carried out at the Nazi concentration camp, Auschwitz. While the atrocities of Auschwitz are worthy of a lifetime of grief, the history of Poland, both current and medieval, is far too robust to be constrained to a point in history where the ethics of common man were turned upside down. Through simple research, one can find that the beauty of Poland is found in the entity that was most affected by the horrors of World War II: its people.

Poland boasts a robust history spanning back to the first recorded event in Polish history in the year 966 BC. Adding to the mystery of the country, the history before this time is largely founded on the legends and folklore that have emanated from the numerous groups of people whose family names survive to this day. A small country, Poland only occupies 120,733 square miles, all of which are divided into administrative subdivisions. The climate of Poland is usually temperate, adding to the beauty of the countryside. Despite its status as a small country with regards to land mass, Poland has populated its small land mass with nearly 39 million people, making it the fifth-largest population in the European Union. The center of Polish government is found in the capital city of Warsaw while the commerce of Poland is supported by other cities such as Kraków, Szczecin, Gdańsk, Poznań, and Łódź. Most Polish commerce is supported by the close proximity of the Baltic Sea while other commerce is supported by the neighboring European nations.

Polish history is a bit of a mystery to the Polish people with the recorded establishment of Poland dating back to 966 BC. The legend surrounding this date involves a king who was once a pagan but converted to Christianity and adopted the emblems of Christianity. While Poland as a country was established in 966, it would not be until AD 1025 that the Kingdom of Poland was founded. The most successful and famous union in Polish history is its unity with Lithuania, which would come over five hundred years later in 1569. The result of this union was the Polish-Lithuanian Commonwealth, a union that effectively quadrupled the size of Poland overnight. The union fashioned a superpower of Europe, the result being a combined population that began immediately pressing for a constitution. It would be another two hundred years before the first constitution in Europe would be written on May 3, 1791.

Poland's supremacy as a nation was tested during the 18th century when the country was divided from Lithuania, crippling the economy and growth of both countries. This separation would last almost one hundred years until the eventual Treaty of Versailles would position Poland once again as an independent country. The season of independence allowed Poland to be a driving force within the commerce, economy, and politics of Europe. This season did not last long though as Poland was among the first European nations to be invaded during the march of World War II. After Poland endured the invasion of its borders by Germany in late 1939, the Soviet Union would subsequently invade Poland, following through on their regulations as outlined in the Molotov-Ribbentrop Pact. The devastation of World War II on Poland as a nation would cripple the country with an estimated six million Polish individuals dying during the war. Of these six million citizens, three million were Jews that fell prey to the march towards a "perfect race" as outlined by Adolph Hitler. Poland would eventually regain its independent status but not before virtually every citizen of Poland paid the price for both Poland's strategic location and Jewish occupancy.

The two largest blights in the history of Poland are found in the horrors of World War II: the Warsaw ghetto and the Auschwitz concentration camp. While the horrors of these camps will be further investigated in the chapter titled "The Modern History of Poland," the horrors cannot be adequately described in such a short manner. The Warsaw ghetto would go down in history as the largest ghetto that the Nazis established, housing 460,000 Jews during the height of its existence. The Warsaw ghetto acted as a holding location for Jews when the prison camps became inundated with the Jews that were being brought in by train from around Europe. When the housing in the ghetto reached its capacity, the Germans proceeded to overfill the rooms, eventually adding up to nine people per room until the end of the war. The highest expedition of ghetto residents took place in 1942, when almost 254,000 residents were sent to their deaths at the Treblinka extermination camp. The Germans were able to accomplish much of this under the very nose of the other European countries by labeling the transportation of Jews by train car as "resettlement in the East." At the bidding of some of its residents, the exporting of residents from the ghetto would be stopped before the war was over when a period of resistance known as the Warsaw Ghetto Uprisings threatened the lives of the German soldiers. Eventually, the Warsaw ghetto was destroyed at the hands of the Germans following the war. In total, over 300,000 people died while being held at the Warsaw ghetto. At the time of its closing, 92,000 people survived within the ghetto, all of which were dismissed to remake their lives in the broken country.

Perhaps the more tragic of the two World War II locations within Poland, the Auschwitz concentration camp would claim over 1.1 million individuals during the war. While Jews were the highest concentration of the individuals being held at these camps, there were also numerous people being held simply because they aided the Jewish people in some manner. Auschwitz was comprised of forty camps that operated as both concentration camps and extermination camps. The camps were mostly outfitted with gas chambers and laboratories to conduct experiments on the Jewish people. Auschwitz would become known to many as the Final Solution to the Jewish Question as outlined by the Nazis. Ironically, the roots of the Auschwitz prison camp were not found in the holding of Jews but rather German criminals. In 1940, the first load of prisoners would come into the camp while the first planned extermination of Polish and Soviet individuals took place in August 1941. While the occurrences at this camp may have been unnoticed by the other European countries, it was well-known to the Polish people what was happening at this camp. Prisoners were often beaten, seldom fed, and occasionally killed simply because the prison had run out of room for all of its occupants. There was no care and no compassion for any of the occupants of this prison. Perhaps the most excruciating detail of this camp were the numerous individuals who were unfortunate enough to become test specimens for the medical experiment labs of the German doctors. The German doctors were not against testing their own people, but towards the end of the war, the test subjects pool was completely comprised of Jewish individuals. There would be numerous uprisings during the history of Auschwitz, but sadly, none would be as successful as the Ghetto Uprisings. To this day, the largest blight on Poland remains its shared responsibility for not destroying the concentration camp. While the Allies would eventually be made aware of the atrocities of this camp, there would be no actions taken against the concentration camp until near the end of the war.

While the Warsaw ghetto and the Auschwitz concentration camp remain demoralizing margins of Polish history, the years following the war would focus on rebuilding the country. The strength of the Polish people grew in correlation with the amount of restoration needed, vaulting Poland to the status as a developed market and the most powerful country in its region of Europe. Today, the Polish economy has transitioned into being the sixth-largest within the European Union and has become an economy embraced by its residents, as denoted by Poland's impressive Human Development Index rating. As a country, Poland has dedicated a large amount of its resources to the education, prosperity, and living conditions of its residents. Poland is one of the few countries to offer free education that ranges from elementary school through university education while also offering free health care for its residents. Poland has taken special care to preserve the numerous national monuments that spot its geography, achieving UNSECO protection on sixteen World Heritage sites.

Politically, Poland exists as a representative democracy led by a president who acts as head of state. The true power of the country, however, would lie with the prime minister, who is considered the head of the Council of Ministers. Poland has joined the United Nations, the European Union, and NATO, all segments which boost the country's economics and trading platforms. The official language of Poland is Polish, and as a country, Poland's primary ethnicity is comprised of Polish individuals. With only 3% of its land mass represented by water, Poland is able to offer adequate housing and land to its 39 million residents. In 2019, Poland's GDP per capita was $17,369, sliding the country into 54th place globally.

As a country, Poland has endured the heartbreak, tragedy, and loss that few other countries have felt; however, it has also been able to promote growth that few countries can achieve. As a nation, Poland has a close-knit residency that is primarily comprised of families. Through the history of Poland, one can learn that while the choices leading to a blight, such as World War II, brought on Poland were one man's actions, the response and growth from that blight will always be the choice of the people. Poland chose to respond to its tragedy with a tremendous rebuilding effort and one that has resulted in the powerful nation Poland is today.

THE FIRST DAYS OF POLAND

The earliest known inhabitants of Poland were found during the Bronze and Iron Age. These people were known as the Biskupin and occupied a fortified settlement, the ground of which is now one of Poland's sixteen UNESCO sites. Polish history from 400 BC until AD 500 was dominated by various ethnic groups that primarily stayed in their own region of the land mass now known as Poland. Various ethnicities included Germanic, Baltic, Scythian, Celtic, and Sarmatian groups. In addition to these groups, there is strong proof that various Roman Legions also made the land of Poland a common place to stage strategic attacks or rest from attacks. It is believed that during this time, the Roman government sent out various groups to explore land mass as far as they could. Many of these Roman groups made it to Poland but failed to ever claim the land for the Roman government. While there is no Roman record of such occurrences, the journals and historical records from numerous Slavic groups explains gatherings of such people. Within the 6th century in the common era, the Slavic people were the primary ethnic group of Poland, occupying the land under a pagan religion that did not tolerate any function of Christianity. In the few years prior to the Middle Ages, Poland's shape began to form.

In the middle of the 10th century, the religion of the Slavic people inhabiting what is now Poland had been paganism. That would change shortly after with an event now known as the Baptism of Poland. During this moment, the leaders of the small government in Poland transitioned from paganism to a full embrace of Western Christianity. Specifically, the leaders began supporting the religious thoughts of the Roman Church, causing quite a stir among the people. The individuals who had so long practiced paganism under the protection of their leaders were now being requested to transition to a new and completely adverse religion: Christianity. While the leaders of the country would transition to a new religion seemingly overnight, it would still be over a hundred years before the rest of the citizenry fully accepted the religious transition. Although the full acceptance of the new religion might have been years away, something much bigger was beginning to take place in the country: the formation of formal government.

Poland's first "true" government was established under the watchful eye of the Piast dynasty. With keen attention to the growing faction of citizens in the country, the Piast dynasty began laying the foundation for the creation of a territorial augment of government within the mid-900s. The man responsible for this transition to a more formalized government was the same man who had led Poland in its transition from paganism to Christianity: King Mieszko I. After the official Baptism of Poland in 966 in which the Catholic fathers formally recognized Poland as a Christian nation, the religious transition began to slowly seep into the population. After King Mieszko passed away, his son Boleslaw the Brave saw to it that his father's dream of a Christian nation was carried out. To facilitate this acceptance, Boleslaw attempted to hold a meeting, the Congress of Gniezno, where the metropolis of Gniezno was formulated. With the metropolis created, Boleslaw met his father's expectations with the creation of dioceses in Kraków, Wroclaw, and Kolobrzeg. Boleslaw would die before this creation was complete, leaving the legacy of his father to be carried out by his successor, Casimir I the Restorer. Whereas the people of Poland had simply been resistant towards accepting the new factions of their new religion under both Mieszko and Boleslaw, the people actually mounted a resistance against Casimir I the Restorer, resulting in the subsequent transfer of the capital city from Gniezno to Krakow. This uprising from those still adhering to paganism in Poland would act effectively as a large roadblock to the future of Christianity in the nation, and for the time being, no more talk of religious transition was made by the kingdom.

The successor to Casimir I, Prince Boleslaw III Wrymouth, held perhaps the most important battle of this time period when he led a conquest against King Henry V of Germany, meeting the German army at the Battle of Hundsfield, where Prince Boleslaw was victorious. This defeat of the German army was key as the German army had been attempting an advance into the Polish countryside. The details of the battle were so great that their full stories are measured in the 1118 Chronicle by Gallus Anonymus. Shortly before Prince Boleslaw died, he dissected his land among his sons, creating numerous duchies that would be ruled by each son.

Over one hundred years after the countryside of Poland was split into numerous factions by Boleslaw, the reigning Duke of the Piast dynasty, Konrad I of Masovia, mounted a campaign to fight against the Baltic Prussian pagans who were seeking to disrupt the Christian transition of the Polish people. By now, most of the Polish population had transitioned to Christianity; however, the Polish government was still worried that the dissenters within the fringe of paganism that still existed might act as an impediment to the future growth of Christianity. With this in mind, Konrad I of Masovia reached out to the Teutonic Knights for aid in the fight against the Baltic Prussian Pagans. While the Baltic Prussian Pagans would eventually be defeated, it would not be for an additional three centuries, leaving the Polish and the Teutonic Knights in constant warfare for almost three centuries.

Perhaps the most afflicted people group within Poland is the Jews, most notably afflicted during the World War; however, their affliction goes back centuries. In 1264, the General Charter of Jewish Liberties was not pleased that its people were being treated so ill in Poland. Thus, a resulting document from this time period granted a list of rights that Jewish people were given. While the Jewish people were now protected by the rights afforded in this new document, the document served as the largest barrier between the people groups of Poland, effectively shunning the Jewish people from the other ethnic groups within Poland.

To this point in the history of Poland, the majority of Poland was comprised of numerous people groups. While this allowed for autonomy among the different people groups, there was a looming lack of unity among the people. The 13th century brought new kings into the kingdom, all of which tried to unite these different Polish groups. Under the mantra of strength through unity, king after king futilely attempted to unite these different groups. The greatest attempt at unity came from the Silesian branch within the Piast dynasty. This branch was ruled by Henry I the Bearded and Henry II the Pious, and the unity of these nations was almost reached; however, the Mongols noticed the distracted people and decided to attack the Eastern portion of Poland. The kings had no choice but to retreat from the construction of a unified people group in order to defeat the advancing Mongols. As it would turn out, the Mongols had timed their advance against the Polish people perfectly, defeating the Polish Army at the Battle of Legnica. While the loss was a severe defeat within itself, the greater defeat was the loss of Duke Henry II the Pious. For the next one hundred years, the Polish kingdom would slowly split apart, each king futilely attempting to unite the kingdom. With each king, it seemed the desire to unite was shared by fewer people. However, in the year 1320, King Wladyslaw, a highly influential noble, used the full force of his power to overtake the throne and become king. Today, he is remembered as the first king that sat upon the throne of a unified kingdom within Poland. Additionally, this is considered the Golden Age within Polish history, as the country became unified for the first time. When Wladyslaw passed from the throne, his son, Casimir III, reigned in his stead. Casimir III is remembered as being the greatest Polish king, primarily for his attention focused on creating an infrastructure that was supposed to withstand many of the attacks that the neighboring countries might place on Poland. Casimir III was a strong proponent of protections for the Jewish people, going as far as to encourage their continual immigration to Poland.

With Casimir III increasing the rights of every Jewish person to the same standard as most Polish citizens, Jews began coming to Poland in droves. With a keen eye on the future growth of Poland, Casimir III began laying the foundation for a group of highly skilled educators to create a school for higher learning, the modern-day equivalent of a university. Casimir's primary purpose in creating this institution of learning was to educate future lawyers and politicians who could write laws for the country. The result of Cssimir's desire was the University of Krakow, the first formal learning center hosted by the government and approved by Pope Urban V. To this point in Polish history, the governing body of Poland had always been the Piast dynasty. To spread the governing bodies slightly, Casimir helped create the Golden Liberty given to the nobles of his day. The Golden Liberty entailed the protections offered to nobles who offered their military service to the kingdom. At the conclusion of their military term, these nobles were granted the status of superior nobleman, a status that placed them far above the status of the common man. The plan worked, for Casimir always had a strong supply of nobles to fight in his army. In 1370, the most beloved king in the history of Poland died when Casimir passed away. The succession for kingdom was complicated by the fact that Casimir did not have a male heir who could take his place as king. As such, the Piast dynasty, the first major ruling body of Poland, came to an end. Thus would end the early history of Poland.

When one looks at the early history of Poland, it is easy to see the infrastructure taking shape as the Middle Ages were beginning to take full effect. When the Piast dynasty came to its end, Poland was growing in unity and becoming the primary destination for Jews in search of equal rights. The coming days of the Polish kingdom would hold more battles but a greater sense of unity than the country had ever known.

THE END OF
THE MIDDLE AGES IN POLAND

With Casimir III creating a common path for all immigrants to follow into Poland, the ethnic groups of the Jews and even German, Flemish, Scottish, Danish, and Walloon immigrants flooded into the land. While the years from 1347-1351 created a large loss of life for most of Europe with the Black Death harvesting death after death, Poland was able to avoid the disaster for the most part, some historians pointing to the royal decree to quarantine the borders of the country as being the largest influential factor in Poland's avoidance of the plague. While the true cause of this avoidance will never be known, this time did help usher in the next dynasty of Poland: the Jagiellon dynasty. The first leader of this dynasty would be the Grand Duke of Lithuania, Wladyslaw II Jagiello. This king would unite the two kingdoms of Poland and Lithuania, giving both countries access to some of the best resources that the respective nation was able to create as a core commodity. Additionally, the union gave both countries a greater array of weaponry and defense should any of the other European countries create hostility between the nations. This union between the two nations would continue for four centuries following the beginning of the Jagiellon dynasty.

Recalling the days when the Mongol army invaded Poland, one would remember that Poland reached out to the Teutonic Knights for their support and defenses. While this prevented the Mongols from advancing further into the country, it did create a problem when the Teutonic Knights continued fighting, this time setting their sights on the Polish Army. The constant struggle between these nations had continued for almost three centuries until a fateful day in 1410 when the newly combined forces of the Polish-Lithuanian army handed the Teutonic Knights one final loss. Almost fifty years later, another decisive victory took place in 1466 when the Thirteen Years' War ended with the subsequent Duchy of Prussia. During this time, the Polish force of power was at its peak, helping check the advances of numerous nations surrounding the country. Among the nations affected by Poland's large army were Bohemia, the Ottoman Empire, and Hungary. The battles between the Ottoman Empire and the Polish Army were by far the most extensive, a recorded seventy-five battles taking place between 1474 and 1569. While the Polish Army was quick to check the advances of most of its enemies, a serious problem developed when the Crimean army began making slave runs against the people along the shore of Poland and Lithuania. In all, it is speculated that over 1 million citizens of Poland were lost in the numerous slave attacks that terrorized the coastline. While the attacks on slaves would eventually end, the Polish people suffered a great deal under the inability of the Polish Army to curb these attacks.

Under the watchful eye and guidance of the Jagiellon dynasty, the government of Poland began to develop into a successful feudal system. The growing agricultural scene of the country provided it with one of the fastest growing economies of the day. Under the rule of Casimir III, the period of Golden Liberty had begun. This focus on nobility took new importance in the 1500s when a new act from Parliament titled the Nihil Novi Act shifted the power from the kingdom to the existing parliament of Poland. This parliament was comprised of the nobles who had previously served in the military and were not eligible to receive their status as men better than the common man. At its peak, the motto of the Sejm was "Free and Equal," denoting that the individuals below the Sejm were all equal. Those who know their history will also recognize this time as it corresponds with the Protestant

Reformation, a time of revival in Christianity as sparked by Martin Luther in Germany. Until this point, Christianity had been the state religion of Poland, having replaced paganism centuries earlier. With the new focus on religious liberty, Poland followed the lead of numerous other nations in allowing its citizens the ability for religious freedom and religious tolerance. Once again, Poland observed the strife taking place in other European countries where the people's voices were not heard and made political decisions based on such research. It was through this that Poland was able to mitigate the dissension within its country.

In the late 1540s, the European Renaissance began to seep into Poland, resulting in new thoughts on science and education. With the new focus on education and learning, Poland began opening new trade routes, resulting in a surge within the Polish economy. As the economy of Poland began to swell, the cultural benefits of Poland also began to increase to the point that Poland was seen as a very inviting culture and the increase in immigration showed such sentiment. Perhaps the greatest contribution of Poland during the European Renaissance was through science when Polish astronomer Nicolaus Copernicus levied his assertion of a heliocentric world in his book On the Revolutions of the Celestial Spheres. The period of the renaissance within Poland would reach its climax in 1569 when the country passed the Union of Lublin, which effectively established the Polish-Lithuanian Commonwealth. While the two countries had been brought together under previous monarchies, this new agreement was a more formal means of identifying the union between the countries and also allowed the officials to be regularly elected within an elective monarchy. The primary goal of the establishment of the commonwealth was the creation of a central parliament to govern both countries. After the union was created, there would be subsequent political meetings where further legal establishment would be outlined, such as the Warsaw Confederation in 1573 where the religious freedoms of the Polish people were agreed upon. In total, the Union of Lublin created a joined entity responsible for over one million square miles of countryside.

When the union between Poland and Lithuania was first formally recognized, the stability within the two governments was almost surprising. One would expect some growing pains; however, the two countries were able to coexist with their formal separations but one joined government. The period of stability would stutter to a halt in the latter months of the 1500s when the formal dynasty rulers of Poland became known for their corruption. Such corruption subsequently led to conflicts with Russia, the Ottoman Empire, and Sweden. Poland would emerge victorious after the various battles with Russia, achieving victory in 1610 when Commander Hetman Stanislaw Zolkiewski was victorious at the Battle of Klushino. One year later, the czar of Russia formally announced his homage, decreeing his succession of the war.

As the union with Lithuania continued to grow older, the formal governing body, once touted by the Golden Liberties espoused upon those who gave of themselves to fighting in the army, began to deteriorate. Largely due to a general sense of greed for more power, the nobles began to trample upon one another, scrambling for even the slightest amount of power. The result was the gradual disintegration of the Commonwealth that had previously been described as the strongest governing body yet. When the Cossack Khmelnytsky Uprising disrupted the lives of the Polish people, the nobles were forced to allow the division of Ukraine, effectively giving the eastern portion of the Ukraine to the Russian government. The rest of the 1600s were entrenched in what is now known as the Deluge, a time when the Swedish army found a vulnerable portion of Poland's population and proceeded to invade the country. As the Swedish army moved forward, they proceeded to ruin farmland and agricultural opportunities, effectively stifling the Polish economy. With the diminished economic strength, the standard of living in Poland plunged, leaving many Polish people sick. Accompanying diseases and starvation would lead to nearly 4 million deaths, a stark number when compared with the usual population of 11 million individuals. In retrospect, the 17th century was the most tumultuous time for Poland yet. With her country now divided and dying, it seemed that the country had perhaps grown beyond what it was able to control. Fortunately for the country, there was a capable individual who was up to the task of reunifying the country.

John III Sobieski would be remembered as the man who was perfect for the job at hand: reunifying a country that was suffering from a loss of morale. The first moment of victory in a while would take place in 1683 when John III Sobieski would lead his forces against the Ottoman Army at the Battle of Vienna. In this army, the victorious courage of the Polish Army was re-established and the citizens of the country finally had something to be proud of. For the time being, Poland was once again the growing power it had been before the Deluge.

Even with the return to power, the power vacancy within Poland was evident to anyone watching from the outside. Historians consider this time period as being the end of the golden age that had vaulted Poland to one of the superpowers of the day in Europe. Perhaps the most significant contributing issue was the feeling that Poland was constantly at war with someone. As these battles continued to wage on, internal strife began to emanate from the kingdom, many people unsure that fighting battles was the best way to restore the kingdom to its former glory. This fall from the golden age would be marked by the terrible rulership of the kings during this time. With the country falling apart, the kings resorted to shady business dealings and an even more inconspicuous legislative process that passed a number of laws that directly hindered the citizens of Poland. On a number of occasions, the people of Poland rose up in anger against the Polish government, staging various uprisings such as the Lubomirski Rebellion. Before long, the highest governing body in Poland would be operated by numerous magnates instead of kings. While this may have seemed like a trivial disagreement or even growing pains, it was sadly laying the foundation for a glorious division of the country. As Poland continued its spiral from glory, Russia began harvesting the victories of this fall, gathering key victories at locations such as the Great Northern War. On the heels of this destruction, the Polish people pushed for reform in their society, a measure granted by Parliament with the ushering in of the Age of Polish Enlightenment. The beginning of the 1700s marked a time period in which the Parliament attempted various measures of societal reform; nonetheless, the people were not satisfied with merely an attempt at reform. As the multiple attempts at social reform fell on deaf ears, other transitions within the country began to take place, the most notable being the moving of the capital from Gdansk to Warsaw. While the country may have been drifting away from its prestigious and prosperous roots, there was no doubt that the divide was truly coming between the nobles and the common citizens of the day. Many nobles were able to maintain strong incomes during this time, often harvesting the lower-priced goods of their befallen countrymen. Sadly, this divide would lead to an even further division of the country. It has been said that great countries are not divided from the outside but rather from within. If only the Polish people could have seen the injurious future that was laying before them; however, none had the foresight to see such a moment and the terrible days that lay ahead rushed into the country with no warning, setting the country into a time now known as the Partition of Poland.

THE EARLY MODERN HISTORY OF POLAND

In 1764, Poland held a royal election in which the country gave the monarchy to a young man named Stanislaw II August. The primary influence resulting in his election was his connection to the groups of magnates that had been operating the country for the past hundred years. Perhaps of more concern was this man's allegiance to Russia, a factor that he held would not influence his decisions as king but an allegiance that he was nonetheless unwilling to break. In 1768, the Bar Confederation was formed and fueled the rebellion in protest of the Polish government, specifically the surmised traitor Stanislaw II. The goal of the rebellion was to remove the king and maintain the independence of Poland as had been outlined in the previous government. As a precursor to the division that would eventually rob Poland of its union with Lithuania, a dissolution of the union was begun as early as 1772 when an activity known as the First Partition of Poland took place. In this time, King Stanislaw II was attempting to bid Austrian aid that would have helped Poland loose itself from its Russian shackles. Unfortunately, the bid for war was rejected when the partition was passed by Frederick the Great as his response to the Austrian's rumor of war. With Frederick the Great being king of Prussia, fear sank into the hearts of the Polish people as they wondered if their country would be taken over. With the partition official, only time would tell if the Polish people were able to rescue their country.

As the news of the partition set in throughout the countryside, the government of Poland refused to pay attention to the partition, instead using this time to create the Commission of National Education. This commission led to increased standards of living throughout the country, namely barring anyone from subjecting a child to the same corporal punishment of their adult peers. Parliament reconvened in 1788 under the title of the Great Sejm, and work was set out to completely overhaul the current government infrastructure. Under the leadership of the Great Sejm, a constitution was written, aptly titled the May 3 Constitution. This constitution would go down in history as being the first laws that governed a nation supremely in Europe. While the new laws within the constitution seemed to settle the political landscape of Poland, civil unrest soon sprang up, the citizens concerned that there were laws within the constitution that were intended to aid those in favor of a revolution and the dissolution of the union between the Lithuanian government and Poland. With the country rising in strong unrest, the Russian government saw this as an opportunity to attack the country while vulnerable and promptly invaded Poland. This would begin the Polish-Russian War.

At first, the Polish people, incensed by Russia's bravery in invading the country, were sure they would win the war, and fighting against the Russians was considered an honor; however, this courage soon turned to further disgust and anger when King Stanislaw II abdicated from his position as king and joined the very forces that were destroying his country. With no king on the throne, the Bar Confederation assumed the throne and sought to orchestrate a war. The transition to power by the confederation was actually a strong move on the part of the Polish people. Immediately, the Russian forces were concerned that they would no longer be able to defeat the newly inspired Polish Army, thus prompting the Russians and Prussians to come together to execute a second partition, officially known as the Second Partition of the Commonwealth. While the first partition sought to remove the union between Lithuania and Poland, this partition sought to cramp

Poland's living spaces to the point that the people were unable of living without the aid of the Russian government. Two years of horror would follow for the Polish people, who, in their gasp for freedom, were unable to quell the forces of Russia. After the two years had passed, the Russian government passed one final partition, and with one final blow, dissolved the commonwealth between Lithuania and Poland. Poland had effectively been surrounded by its neighbors, at which point it was forced to give up its supremacy as a kingdom and return to its original land mass size.

Immediately following the third partition, the Polish people mounted a small resistance against those seeking to partition the country. One such uprising was known as the Kościuszco Uprising, a particularly valiant effort from a man who had previously served within the ranks of George Washington during the Revolutionary War in the United States of War. While this uprising had victories, the end would be a miserable defeat for Poland and one final defeat: Poland was no longer a free country. With the government in shambles, neighboring countries moved in to overtake the throne or set up various governments within the country. One such government was France, governed by the courage of Napoleon I who created the Duchy of Warsaw. This occupancy by France would last only until the end of the Napoleonic Wars, after which the country would once again fall and return to its divided state. Within the eastern portion of the divided country, Poland had fallen into the hands of the Russians who ruled the Congress Poland. The western portion of Poland, once controlled by the Prussians, would eventually fall into the hands of the Germans. The divide between the two portions of the country became quite different. While Polish people were granted their freedoms in the western portion of the country, the eastern portion of the state began to adopt more and more Russian government until the country was barely noticeable as a former Polish country.

Even as they watched their country become more and more like their governing nations, the citizens of Poland refused to go without a fight. Thus, it was not uncommon for the Russian, Prussian, and Germanic troops to be met with fierce resistance. While this resistance did little to stamp out the fire of the occupying countries, it was a good reminder to the people of Poland that their voices were still being heard. In 1830, the Polish forces combined in Warsaw where they were commanded by Lieutenant Piotr Wysocki. The location of Warsaw was strategic due to the Officer Cadet School being formed there. After a series of meetings in which the cadets were rallied to courage against the Russian troops occurring their city, a faction of Polish citizens joined these cadets in revolting against the Russians. The battle, for now, was successful with the Russian troops chased out of the city and to the north. While the cadets knew that the Russians would be back with more troops, it was an encouragement to know that they still were capable of standing for what they believed in. This particular uprising would become known as the November Uprising. The Russians would fail to secure Warsaw again for the next seven months, during which the Polish forces were able to defend the city heroically. With the Polish people mounting an offensive against the overarching powers of the Russian government, the Polish government attempted to secure the additional protection and troops that the neighboring countries had; however, the neighboring countries were none too eager to give troops to Poland. With no power, the Polish drive for victory disappeared into the night. The following day, Warsaw would be surrendered to the Russians, and days later, almost the entire Polish Army ran east where they crossed into the lands occupied by the Prussian troops and surrendered. With no defense, Poland was once again aligned with the Russian government, never before appearing to be so closely related. At the time, it seemed that Poland was destined to become a part of Russia, never to return to its independence.

For over fifteen years, the Polish people remained in subjection to the Russian government. There seemed to be very little hope that the Polish people could ever reinvent themselves as a country and inspire their people to fight again. However, as the Polish people grew angrier with their current state, various voices began calling for a new revolution. The result would be a new time of revolts named the Spring of Nations. The Polish people began scraping together whatever weapons they could find, joining in what would eventually be known as the Greater Poland Uprising of 1848. While the uprising began as a small group of Polish farmers who were attempting to create a skirmish with troops, the Prussian army exacerbated the party when it came crashing into the affair, killing several of the Polish troops. The result would be a renewed battle against the Prussian army but would sadly not last long. The Polish people were able to keep the Prussian army on the move for several days, but once again, without the access to resources such as the Prussian army had, there was no possible way the Polish Army could maintain the resistance. After surrounedring yet again, the Polish Army returned home in humility, the new Grand Duchy promising to be harsher than the previous king had been.

The next eleven years would see the Polish people attempt to live on their meager rations and in terrible living conditions. In 1863, however, the Polish people had a new voice that once again called for reform and a renewed battle against the Russian troops. With a new sense of courage, the Polish people began gathering weapons, and the January Uprising took root. The early days of the January Uprising saw it emerge as a group of Polish people merely trying to antagonize the Russian troops that maintained their presence in Poland. As more people joined the daily antagonizing of the troops, however, the two groups began sparring more frequently, and soon, a new war had erupted on the Polish front. When the Russian army began gathering young Polish men to fight in the Russian army, the battle broke out in a new rage. While the Polish troops were no match for the thousands of Russian troops, the Polish Army tried to fight with more than troops, often sitting ambushes for the Russian troops or resorting to assassinations. The Russians would best the Polish troops in every battle of this uprising, the Polish troops' lack of organized fighting coming back to destroy the attempted attacks. At the conclusion of this uprising, it was decided that no future uprisings should be held since the past few uprisings had failed to gather any momentum. Rather than destroy the Russian troops, the Polish people set out to improve their standard of living as best they could. Poland would be able to add factories to the country, and the people of Poland watched as their country's economy suddenly blossomed amidst the tragedy of the Russian occupancy. The Polish people set their mind to the task at hand, industrializing their nation, and by the end of the 19th century, the country was a fellow competitor for goods.

As the world turned one century older, Poland retained its status as an occupied country and failed to operate its government as its own. The beginning of the 20th century was calm, but the rising political unrest in the late 1920s seemed to signal that something much larger was coming. While the Polish radicals had attempted to curb any future uprisings given the grim outlook of overthrowing the Russian government, there were still voices that called for resistance. As the political unrest in Europe continued to grow, the rest of the world suddenly became involved, most major countries issuing statements on their stance regarding Poland's independence. None of these voices were stronger than the voice of Woodrow Wilson, who proclaimed that Poland should once again be granted its own constitution. This proclamation was made in the middle of President Wilson's famous fourteen points speech and caused ripples around the world. In a subsequent uprising in 1918, the Polish troops were able to gather some semblance of organization, going as far as to prompt Germany to agree to their armistice the same year. With the armistice signed, Poland made preparations to once again become independent. Finally, after years of fighting and numerous uprisings, Poland was able to proclaim its independence, officially recognized as the Second Polish Republic.

The fight for independence was not over yet, as Vladimir Lenin still attempted to bring his power of Communism throughout Europe. When Russia began antagonizing the Polish troops, the impending war was called the Polish-Soviet War. This war would last from 1919 until 1921 when the Polish Army had its second great win in three years, defeating the daunting Red Army at the Battle of Warsaw. To this day, the heroic efforts of the Polish Army are remembered as the Miracle at the Vistula. While the battle engrained victory in the hearts of the Polish people, it also served to cease the spread of

Communism throughout Europe, acting as a key blocker against Russia's goal of global domination.

With the country back in formation, the government of Poland set out to regain all of the land that it had been stripped of during the various partitions. During this time, Poland also paid special attention to the formation of transit within the country, laying rail lines that ran directly into the capital cities so that the commerce of Poland could flourish. To further charge the emerging economy, Poland also established a port on the Baltic Sea that allowed ships to bring their goods to Poland while also allowing the export of Polish goods. As the country was reopening from the horrors of its partitions, the voices of Poland were strengthened by the emergence of several key individuals who had held prominent positions prior to the dissolution of the Polish-Lithuanian union. In 1922, the growth of the country was momentarily halted upon the tragic assassination of the current president of Poland, Gabriel Narutowicz. The politics of the country would continue to face several transformations over the next few years as constant attention had to be paid to the various radical groups that wanted to see Poland removed from its stable pedestal. As these radical groups continued to grow in number, the Polish government was forced to relax some of its lenient policies, following the example set by other nations in banning several radical organizations. In 1938, one year before the greatest tragedy to befall Poland would occur, Poland was gifted a small tract of land from Czechoslovakia, an act of good will and one that would bring the two countries together.

While the Polish people were proud to once again be a nation that was respected by the world, there was still a nagging feeling within many of them that the Russians were being far too quiet. Truly, the Polish people had no idea what horrors awaited them in the following year. In just one year, Poland would embark on a journey that would test the will of every citizen. Truly, the following time period would test the will of most of the world: that time period was none other than World War II.

THE MODERN HISTORY OF POLAND

While no nation desires to be at war, its existence is inevitable. Often, war is considered the last result in an expedition of attempted coercion or influence. Even as a nation at war desires to win the war, there is a stronger desire that hinges around not being invaded. There is somewhat of a crippling effect when a nation is invaded. Such was true for Poland on September 1, 1939. Poland had long been brewing in its hostility towards Germany. Poland had attempted to gain back some of the land that had been taken from it during the partitions; however, with a new man at the helm in Germany, it seemed that all hope was gone for Poland ever seeing that land again. This man, Adolf Hitler, spoke of wanting to unite the world; however, many were quick to see through his facade of unity into the core of a man who merely wanted to rid the world of any threat to the Aryan race. Poland would become the battlegrounds for the war as the Soviet Union followed Germany's lead into Poland, invading from the other side of the country less than one month later. Eleven days after Poland had been effectively surrounded by its enemies, the capital city of Warsaw became the latest victim in the march of Adolph Hitler. In a subsequent meeting which produced the Molotov-Ribbentrop Act, the country of Poland was once again divided, this time with the Germans and Soviets splitting the country equally. The Polish people would suffer tremendously under the leadership of their respective zones before eventually being deported from their own country. The Soviet army proved to be the worst of the two occupancies during this time, shooting and killing hundreds of Polish people while continuing to lead the charge towards removing Polish people from the country. By November of the same year, the German army was reading propaganda that called for the complete annihilation of the Polish people. While this would never happen, millions of Polish people would lose their life in the coming days.

The German and Soviet occupancy of Poland proved to be of utmost value to the Allies, who relied on the spies within the country who could tell of Soviet or German military advances. Eventually, in an act that would lead to the end of World War II, Polish physicists would be the primary influencers in a project that interpreted the codes from the Enigma, a sophisticated coding operative as given by the German army. For the time being however, the Polish influence within the country as mere spies was valuable enough. With the country effectively split in two, the Polish Army would hold different allegiances during this time. While some served as troops within the Polish government in the western portion of Poland, the rest actually served the Soviet government in the east. With the numerous battles that would take place during this war, the Polish troops proved to be invaluable to whatever side they were fighting on. One battle of importance is the Battle of Monte Cassino. Additionally, heroic battles such as the Normandy Invasion, the Italian Campaign, and the North African campaigns would likely have held different outcomes had the war not had the support of Polish troops. After all, when combined, the Polish troops constituted the fifth-largest army in Europe. While the Polish people disliked having the Soviets in their country, the Soviet army did provide troops for the Polish Army, leaving the Polish government content to focus on the German invasion and the subsequent attempts at removing these troops from their country.

Known as the Armia Krajowa, the Polish Army set out to develop a sophisticated world underneath the eyes of the German leadership. While the Polish people appeared to be in compliance with the numerous new laws that the Germans placed on them, the Polish people were actually involved in managing an underground world where all legal battles were settled and higher education took place. The German occupation of Poland took new significance later that year when Adolph Hitler began constructing various prison camps throughout the country. In shocking fashion, some of these prison camps were constructed as extermination camps, locations solely dedicated to the killing of prisoners. Additionally, Germany began establishing ghettos throughout Poland, cities that were dedicated to maintaining prisoners. Often, these ghettos were home to horrors and atrocities as the German soldiers did whatever they pleased with the Polish prisoners. The previous days of the resistance seemed to be over as any Polish individual seen as a threat to the German army or government was either exiled to a prison camp or executed on the spot. The current times were dark for all Polish people, but sadly, the darkest days ahead would be occupied by a select group of people: the Jews from Poland.

One would recall that in previous governments, the Polish kingdom had welcomed the immigration of Jews, leading to a large occupancy of Jews. When Adolph Hitler began his rampant run against the Jews of the world, the Polish Jews were anything by spared from his wrath. In regard to ethic composition of country populations compared before and after the war, it is hard to find a contingency of Jews more affected than the ones in Poland. Today, less than one percent of Poland's population is Jewish, an astounding 90% of the Jewish population falling to the brute of Adolph Hitler. The Jews were not the only people affected though: almost 3 million Polish people would be killed during the early portion of the war. While the loss of life is always a tragedy, it did not help the Polish people when they realized the majority of their doctors, nurses, pastors, and nobility were being killed by the German troops. The troops had been trained to create chaos by killing the leaders of various groups of people. Perhaps the bloodiest battle during this time for the Polish people took place at the Warsaw Uprising, a resistance that was destined for failure from the moment it started. At the conclusion of the massacre, over 150,000 Polish people would be killed. For the Polish people, there was little to no hope that the Germans would ever retreat from their position. With each battle, the Germans seemed to fortify their position in Poland to become even stronger, leading to a loss of morale for the Polish people. Fortunately, while it may have seemed that the Polish people were fighting alone, the truth is that the world was inspired by this small country who refused to be pushed around by the bigger countries. While the country was enduring tragic losses, its voice remained the same, growing stronger with the death of each Polish person.

The Soviet occupation of Poland would be markedly lighter on the Polish population, although 150,000 Polish people would meet their demise under the fists of the Soviet Union. The tragedy of the Soviet Union's occupancy of Poland was Joseph Stalin's decree that led to routine evictions of the Polish people. In all, over 2 million people would be forced to leave Poland, decimating the country's population and defenses while also dividing families. At the conclusion of the war, it would be revealed that of all of the countries involved in the war, Poland would suffer the largest loss per capita. Over 17% of the country's population being killed during the war, an estimated 90% of these deaths coming off the battlefield.

With the war nearing its end, the Soviet Union sought to gather some land before the war was over. As a result, the Oder-Neisse line was created, leading to Poland losing an additional 20% of its land mass. Whereas the country had once been the supreme authority of Central Europe with its union with Lithuania, Poland's population was dwindling as was its land mass. Towards the end of 1944, the Red Army from the Soviet Union began its march towards Auschwitz, resulting in the deportation of thousands of war criminals and prisoners. The deportation would be a death march though as most of these prisoners and criminals would be killed in concentration camps in Germany. In early 1945, the Soviet army reached the most horrific prison camp, Auschwitz, where they were greeted with starving people and a myriad of German soldiers. Eventually, American troops would also enter the camp, giving America its first glimpse of the horrors that Communism had brought to the country. To this day, Poland religiously celebrates January 27 as International Holocaust Remembrance Day.

Prior to the end of the war, the Allies held a meeting at the Yalta Conference during which the leader of the Soviet Union, Joseph Stalin, announced his intention to create a new government in Moscow that would allow the practice of Communism. Such a move was infuriating to the Polish people who were currently seeing their country occupied by two countries, both in the name of Communism. Stalin further infuriated the Polish people by claiming that he had allowed the Polish government complete autonomy during the Soviet occupation of the country. Polish people would soon find that while Stalin did allowed elections, these elections were rigged and handed the power directly to the Soviet Union. With the rigged elections handing power to the Soviet Union, Stalin paid a special visit to Poland in which he outlined a new government that would adhere to Communist principles. Many Polish people refused to accept the terms, greeting the news with a militant response. Nonetheless, the Polish government, feeling trapped against the German army from the rear and the Soviet government from the front, agreed that the Soviet Union would annex the land that had previously belonged to Poland. Additionally, the Polish government accepted the Soviet Union occupancy of Poland with troops, a move that many Polish people considered traitorous. In 1947, the Communist government took over Poland's ruling body, and the Polish People's Republic would eventually be formed. The days following the creation of this governing body were horrific for the Polish people. Anyone who spoke of resistance against the Communist government was imprisoned and likely never heard from again. It took until the end of the 1950s for the first resistance to take place, during which numerous people were freed from prison by the secret militia. These resistances would be small in number but would lead to short bursts of patriotism from those who remembered what Poland used to be like.

While the resistance was often unorganized, a growing movement in the 1980s was the "Solidarity" movement as championed by Lech Walesa. Lech Walesa would eventually win the election as president in 1990, becoming the first member of the Solidarity party to achieve a government position in Poland. The Solidarity movement would achieve fame throughout most of Europe, with many small governments retaking the reins of their leadership with such thoughts. The Solidarity movement would be responsible for destroying the prominence of the Polish United Workers' Party during the 1980s. As the Solidarity movement gained momentum, it would be able to remove many of the Communist bands that had crippled its growth for years. In the coming days, transformation was coming to Poland.

At the turn of the 1990s, the government of Poland began drifting away from its previous roots as a socialist economy into more of a market economy. Immediately after announcing such a change, the Polish economy endured a small recession that was common for countries moving away from the socialist economy. The legacy of Poland would not be cemented until it was able to restore the country to its economic prominence that it had experienced prior to being invaded. By 1995, the country was able to boast a GPD that resembled the country's GDP from before the war began. During this time, Poland also underwent what many consider the second-greatest social reform in the history of the country. Under the watchful eye of Leszek Balcerowicz, the country began passing legislation intended to give more freedom to citizens in the areas of speech, civil rights, political freedoms, and internet censorship. Under the previous government administrations and especially during the wars, Poland had lost much of its freedom and resembled some of the most Communist nations of the day. However, the Polish people had endured enough to not want to ever return to such days, allowing Balcerowicz unprecedented ease in adopting these new freedoms. Additionally, to aid against future attacks or invasions from foreign countries, Poland joined numerous organizations dedicated to world peace such as the United Nations and the European Union. To facilitate greater commerce and trade, Poland joined the Visegrad Group and also became a leading contributor within the North Atlantic Treaty Organization. While Poland would never unite with Lithuania following the partitions, the country did seek to build unity contracts with neighboring nations such as the Czech

Republic and Hungary. By entering into contracts with these two nations, Poland was ensured of having two additional armies at its disposal if a situation such as World War II arose again. Though Poland began the process of joining the European Union in 2003, it would be over one year until it was granted full member status with that privilege coming in May of 2004.

Perhaps the most brilliant move for postwar commerce was the addition of the Schengen Area in 2007. The Schengen is a free-trade agreement that goes above the European Union. While only comprised of countries adhering to the European Union, the Schengen Area is a collection of twenty-six countries within Europe that have deemed passport and other primary forms of identification unnecessary for citizens traveling from country to country. Such a move has facilitated greater commerce as merchants from countries all over Europe are able to ship their goods to other countries without having to abide by normal border control legislation. The only requirement for citizens utilizing the law is a visa that is given out by the home country of that resident. Interestingly, there are four nations, Liechtenstein, Norway, Iceland, and Switzerland that have not joined the European Union yet but maintain active membership in the Schengen Area. In all, the Schengen Area occupies 1,664,911 square miles while also boasting a combined population of 420 million individuals. Such has allowed unprecedented growth in the economies of the member countries.

Though the war was over eighty years prior, the Polish government has made it clear that it intends to never repeat the atrocities that stemmed from the Soviet invasion of Poland in World War II. This has led Poland to focus most of its border patrol on the eastern border of the country, the border that Poland shares with Russia and Ukraine. Today, Poland is the proud creator of what many have referred to as Fortress Europe, a border that is reportedly impenetrable by any ground forces. In a subsequent effort to quell any ideas of invading either Poland or one of its neighboring countries, Poland has established an army combined with the resources of the Czech Republic, Hungary, and Slovakia. The combined army is called the Visegrad Battlegroup and consists of an army of 3,000 troops that are always prepared for a possible battle or hot spot that they could be deployed to. To guard against the eastern neighbors who might be tempted to invade, Poland has done more than construct the Fortress Europe: it has also joined in with Lithuania and Ukraine to form the LITPOLUKRBRIG, a combined army that shares more resources than the Visegrad Battlegroup. With these resources combined, it appears that Poland may be ready to weather any attack that a country foolish enough to attack it would levy.

The politics of Poland had been enjoying a new period of growth until 2010 when the ultimate tragedy struck the Polish government. Whenever a country loses an active member of government, it is a tragedy for both the family of the individual lost and the people of the country who now have to find a new person to sit within that person's former seat. However, when a country loses eighty-nine of its highest ranking government officials, a state of emergency develops within the citizens as the realization that almost one hundred leadership positions were just instantly vacated. Sadly, this is exactly what happened in 2010 when Leah Kaczynski was killed in a plane crash that also killed an additional eighty-nine government employees who were considered vital to the success of the government. The tragedy understandably shook the core of Poland as citizens were aware that their safety and security was now going to be found in an emergency election. Adding to the tragedy of the event, Kaczynski and his team were on their way to a service that was to remember the victims of the Katyn massacre. In all, ninety-six people were on board the plane that would perish when it crashed. While the cause of the wreck would always be disputed, what is known is that the pilots were forced to attempt a landing in dense fog, during which the pilots ventured too close to the neighboring trees and eventually struck one of the trees, demolishing the plane into a giant fireball. During subsequent investigations, the Polish officials would deem that the pilots tasked with flying the aircraft were not fit to be doing so, having neither been trained adequately on flying in regular conditions nor the conditions that were present when the aircraft crashed. As a result of the crash, the pilot program that had produced the pilots flying the president's aircraft was disbanded, and an additional group of military leaders responsible for the oversight of the flying program were forced into resignation by outrage from the Polish citizens. While there are numerous conspiracy theories revolving around an attempted assassination of the president, Polish officials have declared they have yet to find any evidence of this destruction being related to an assassination. Nonetheless, the event remains the most tragic event in the last fifty years of Poland's history and one that will remain a tragedy for the future of Poland.

One year following the tragedy of the plane crash, Poland held elections in which the Civic Platform emerged victorious. One year after these elections, Poland declared its dedication to science with a membership in the European Space Agency. To facilitate more commerce and tourism to the country, Poland joined arms with Ukraine in developing the UEFA European Football Championship in 2012. The event would be created in coordination with the Ukrainian government. This subsequently led to Poland's entrance into the Development Assistance Committee, a group of countries that met to discuss the various ways that a country can help emerging economies in their quest for economic freedom. During this time, the politics of Poland fell under new light with many people impressed with how the country was being operated. Symbolizing this impressive record, the president of Poland in 2014 would be selected for the position of president of the European Council. In the subsequent elections held to occupy his vacant seat, the Law and Justice party of Poland would emerge victorious. The Law and Justice party of Poland has been the leading party advocating for greater investigation into the plane crash that killed the Polish president years earlier. Likewise, many have said the party best represents the middle class of Poland.

When looking at the history of Poland, it is hard to imagine a time period in which some tragedy did not take place. From being forced to partition the country to being invaded and named the central location for such atrocities as Auschwitz and the Warsaw ghetto, Poland has undergone tragedies that few countries will ever embrace. However, Poland has also made itself known as being one of the few countries that could grow from being in the depths of ashes to being near the top of the countries involved in the European Union. Poland is the perfect example of a people group who refused to be taken with the cares of sympathy or victimization. Rather than focus on the atrocities that the country has endured, Poland has always maintained a forward-looking mindset, focused on what the country is capable of creating, not focusing on what they have endured. The history of Poland is a beautiful representation of a people group united in their focus and stronger through the unity that tragedies can bring. In addition to making their country stronger, Poland has also been able to make the world stronger, adding to the equity of the European Union and giving the world an example to follow when looking at developing economies. Poland, a country of so much heartbreak, has emerged as a country of even greater courage, a courage that has developed opportunities few countries can boast of.

THE ECONOMY OF POLAND

In surprising fashion for a country of its size, Poland enjoys an economy whose gross domestic product is large enough to be ranked sixth among nations in the European Union. The country shows no signs of quelling this growth either, and the gross domestic product is set to overtake the fifth position within the European Union in the coming days. When the sectors of Poland are examined closely, it can be seen that the majority of Polish individuals are employed within the tertiary service industry, while an addition 30% are employed in some facet of the manufacturing industry. While Poland's economy was originally supported primarily by the agricultural industry, the percentage of Polish individuals in the agricultural industry has fallen to an all-time low of 10% and shows no promise of being able to maintain this level. Poland's economy is one that could be examined by other countries for practice, its historically low unemployment rate, low debt, healthy trade balance, and an excellent unified attitude among its companies all combining to aid Poland in doing more than surviving the recessions of 2008, an accolade no other country can claim. Indeed, Poland did not merely survive the recession, but they were not even touched by the grasp of the economic downturn. Perhaps somewhat leading to this strong position is Poland's refusal to adopt the Euro as its primary currency, as is the practice with so many other members of the European Union.

Even with a strong economy, Poland is still in a state of transformation. With the country having been a Communist government less than one hundred years ago, there are still numerous plans in place to relieve tension within the economy through government policy. When compared with other countries, Poland once again rises above its small size in the pursuit of exporting. As noted in the high percentage of individuals working for the tertiary services industry, Poland is Central and Eastern Europe's leader in banking. Currently, Poland averages almost thirty-three banks for every 100,000 adults, which gives its citizens easy and varietal access to numerous banks that have been forced to compete on virtually every aspect of the customer journey. To encourage competition within the tertiary services industry, Poland led the way for numerous banks to become privately owned while also funneling necessary capital to banks that were in need of growth to remain afloat. The result has been an industry that remains the lifeblood of Poland today, supporting the business ventures that lead to the high percentage of export and ultimately, an excellent standard of living for the Polish nationals. In today's economy, not only do the Polish citizens benefit from their banking prowess; the rise of the banking sector in Poland has enticed almost forty foreign banks to open doors in Poland, eager to share the market of Polish people eager to invest their money.

While the agricultural industry of Poland was once far greater than it currently is, the industry is still considered one of the leading supporters of the food exports in Europe, with Poland set to lead Europe in the production of food if the growth is maintained. Even with fewer than 10% of its labor force employed in the agricultural industry, Poland's agricultural industry continues to grow and maintains low prices for food in the country. While Poland is known for its delicious chocolate, the country also maintains a name as one of the leading exporters of fish, meat, eggs, and milk.

While the country touts its low unemployment rate and the means by which it weathered the global recession of 2008, much of this strength is due to an export that the country would rather curb than grow: its workforce. With the country focusing on supporting free healthcare, education, and disability pensions, the tax burden on individuals and corporations has led to unprecedented emigration from Poland. As a member of the European

Union, Polish residents are able to leave their country and work elsewhere as they desire, a move designed to facilitate better commerce but that has rather created a labor force deficiency in some countries. Poland is one of those countries, and economists now assert that the only reason Poland was able to leave 2008 unscathed by the economic recession is due to the alarming number of residents who had left the country, thus reducing the burden for the government. In all, nearly 2.5 million residents have left Poland for reasons strictly related to opportunity. For those who leave, better opportunities often exist outside of Poland in neighboring countries, and relocation costs are minimal when compared with the gains from the opportunity. For those who stay, the average pay per employee increases with every employee who leaves the country, leading to a nice trade-off for the vigilant employees. Nonetheless, the lack of workers in Poland, though nice for pay and benefits purposes, has left many companies in dire need of workers while also taxing the government with fewer taxpayers. Even with a strong economy and an unemployment rate that rivals most European countries, Poland has seen its unemployment rate rise to 5.7%, a number in stark comparison with other countries such as the United States where the unemployment rate averages around 4%. To encourage some residents to funnel more of their income back into the economy, Poland recently passed legislation that would allow workers who were younger than 26 years old to refrain from paying any income tax.

While supported primarily by its financial institutions, Poland is also one of the leading countries visited by tourists. With beautiful sites to see in Warsaw and other parts of the country, tourism has aided the economy of Poland tremendously. In 2019, the country enjoyed 21 million tourists who are helping the tourism industry challenge the tertiary services industry for the role of leading industry for the gross domestic product of Poland. Since joining the European Union in 2004, Poland has paid special attention to the tourist attractions the country offers, ensuring that natural heritage sites and other new sites are maintained so that the number of tourists only improves. While many tourists enjoy touring the various sites that were influential in

World War II such as Auschwitz, the most popular tourist destination in Poland is the city of Krakow. With Krakow existing as the former capital of the country, the historical viability of the city is adorned in gold, high arches, and other elements key to the Renaissance period. For tourists desiring to see more culture than tourist destinations, they will find the people of Wroclaw very interesting. The city is known for its residents who are dwarfs, giving tourists the feeling they are reliving medieval history when they enter the city limits. In addition to the people of Wroclaw, tourists often flock to this city for its famous gardens and zoo.

As a country, Poland does not offer an overabundance of museums such as other countries facilitate history from. Rather, Poland has chosen to offer its tourists outside experiences such as mountain climbing, beautiful peaks for skiing, and green valleys full of various food crops. With the country bordered by the Baltic Sea, many tourists also flock to the northern portion of the country to relax on one of the beaches offered by the seaside. Even with the renaissance journey found in Wroclaw, the zoo, and the beaches of the Baltic Sea, many tourists are not content with their visit to Poland without a visit to at least one of the castles remaining in Poland. With over one hundred castles to choose from, the tourists maintain the economy of Poland nicely traveling from castle to castle.

With Poland's economic prowess taking on a national spotlight, many of Europe's largest companies have chosen Poland as their home due to the financial position the country's legislation almost immediately places them in. As a result of their passive legislation, Poland has become the home to almost half of the largest corporations that are from Europe. To facilitate global growth, Poland involves most of its stock trading on the Warsaw Stock Exchange. Today, the largest corporations in Poland are comprised of those within the oil and gas sector while the financial services companies are in close pursuit. With a focus on sustainability, Poland has placed priority on fossil fuel production. Today, Poland remains one of the largest exporters of coal, leading to strategic initiatives worldwide for companies able to obtain Poland's coal at a discount compared to other providers. With the energy market developed when it comes to fossil fuels and sustainability, Poland has recently begun new initiatives that will bring a new focus to renewable energy features. To date, the amount of energy produced by renewable sources is meager; however, the country has placed high projections on comprising 15% of its energy production with renewable energies. Already, construction has begun on numerous windmills and hydroelectric stations around the country.

The economy of Poland is a main component of the country's infrastructure, and likewise, the infrastructure of Poland has seen tremendous growth since it began its postwar phase of growth. The postal system of Poland is one of the earliest in history, remaining in operation since 1558. The postal service has obviously undergone tremendous transformation since this time and almost faced extinction in the early 1700s when the country was forced to remove the postal service due to a conflict with one of the neighboring countries; however, the postal service would emerge again in the 20th century with the resurrection of the country prior to World War I. Fortunately, the timing could not have been better as the military would overtook the rejuvenated postal service to conduct military communication while also scanning for intelligence. Today, Poland's postal service has transformed to meet the growing demand of the world, now including financial transfers and international delivery. In recent days, the postal service has also furnished a means by which to track the packages that are sent domestically. The postal service remains a government operation and is locally referred to as the Polish Post.

While Poland's primary support for the economy comes through its tremendous financial services industry, the country has also been a worthy proponent of science and technology, the most famous scientist in Poland considered to be Nicolaus Copernicus. Copernicus was, of course, the scientist whose revelations about the sun led to an acceptance of the heliocentric theory of planet orientation. Unknown to many, Copernicus was also an economist famous for his quantity theory of money. Another famous Polish scientist who changed the world was Marie Curie, the woman whose groundbreaking work in radiation changed the game for cancer treatments and other scientific efforts. Her research laid the foundations for the Radium Institute that she founded in Poland in 1925. Today, Poland's education has taken the reins of the scientific research industry in Poland. Its four thousand five hundred researchers and forty laboratories constitute Central Europe's largest research center. It is commonplace for every university to have its own research facilities, and coupled with generous government funding, Poland's research continues to cause ripples in the ocean of science around the world.

Poland's economy is also supported by the extensive demographics of the country. In regard to population, Poland's nearly 39 million residents rank eighth among European nations and fifth within the European Union. The population is crammed into the small land mass, giving one hundred and twenty-two residents one square mile on the population density ratio. While the residency of Poland is dense, the country does not project strong growth in the future years, its current fertility rate only coming to 1.44 children per woman. This has been alarming to economists in Poland who have discovered that their median population age has increased steadily in the past decade, currently rising at 41.1 years. However, the death rate remains low with the aging population, and economists are hopeful that immigration will decrease the median age.

THE DEMOGRAPHICS OF POLAND

In regard to population location, the majority of Polish people are centered in urban areas; however, the differential between those living in urban locations has diminished to its current rate of 60% of people living in urban areas with 40% comprising the rural countryside. The ethnic background of Poland has changed considerably over the years, most strikingly during the horrors of World War II. Prior to World War II, the country encouraged and profited from a strong Jewish population. However, the atrocities of World War II all but completely wiped this race of people out of Poland's demographics while also costing a considerable portion of Polish people their lives. If one were to look at a line graph of the Polish population from the 1900s until now, there is a tragic and striking drop from 1938 to 1946. In just eight years, the population of Poland was diminished by almost 50%. Incredibly, Poland's population has grown back to even greater numbers since the war but has since flattened its growth. In most recent studies, a striking 97% of the residents in Poland are Polish with the remaining 3% comprised of a myriad of other ethnicities including German, Silesian, and Kashubian, none of which comprise more than 1.3%.

To date, over 1.5 million people have immigrated into Poland, giving the country strong signals that the economy is attracting foreigners while it slowly regains the trust of its citizens. When looking at the variety of languages offered in Poland, one would be surprised to find that Poland only has one language accepted officially by the government: Polish. Other languages dot the land mass but these languages are usually tribal or restricted to a small people group. Some of these languages include Kashubian, of which only 366,000 people in Poland know how to speak. Poland's predominant religion is Catholicism, with 92.9% of the citizens identifying with the Catholic faith. With an astounding 94.2% of the country being religious, Poland is among the greatest religious nations in Europe. An additional 3% of Polish people identified as not religious or agnostic, giving credence to the long history of religious tradition that has driven much of Poland's innovation. While religion may be an important choice for many in Poland, the practice of religion has seen a tremendous decrease, falling to only 38% in 2019. The Polish people maintain that their country should remain free from an official religion, but the number of people who actively practice their religion has dwindled consistently since the early 1970s. Perhaps the most famous religious individual from Poland was the beloved Pope John Paul II who became the first person with Polish ethnicity to become a pope for the Roman Catholic church. Pope John Paul II would hold this position form 1978 until 2005, one of the longer papacies in history. Among the other religions that have small followings around the country are Protestants, Pentecostals, Christian Orthodox, and Jehovah's Witnesses. While most of Poland hails as devoutly religious or holding some affinity with religion, the country has also shown a minority that is atheist as well. Poland produced men like Casimir Liszinksi, a man who showed his allegiance to proclaiming there was no God and being one of the leading influencers for the new atheistic movement in Europe. While atheism is spreading in other parts of Europe, Poland has seen very little growth in this movement. As a whole, Poland hails as a religious country, tolerant of all religions but primarily adhering to Catholic church doctrines.

Education has for the most part always been a government-regulated entity. In 1773, the government first took control of the education of Poland, establishing the Commission of National Education; however, education had long been the focus of the country dating back to as early as the 12th century.

One of the signs of this dedication to education is found in the Jagiellonian University, a university old enough to rank as the 19th university founded that is still standing today. Its founder, King Casimir III, will forever be remembered as a king who held great affection for the needs of society, his government being responsible for encouraging the immigration of thousands of Jews.

The average Pole begins their educational career path when they turn five or six. The children then begin a road map that takes them from the earliest grade school, "0" all the way through middle and upper education. Of particular interest and different than most educational platforms around the world, Poland requires its schoolchildren to take standardized tests at the end of 6th and 9th grade years. While standardized testing is no new concept to the rest of the world, Poland uses this standardized testing to determine which school and even class these students will attend in the future. For students who fare well on the standardized test, great educational opportunities await them, and often, numerous schools accept the students leading to greater competition among these schools. For students who fail to pass the test in a fashion that distances themselves from the pool of students being recruited by secondary schools, there are still numerous options available for their use, including the lyceum, which is a school that students can attend for three years. During these years, the students will receive a more generic education while students who were selected by secondary school institutions will receive a specialized education that can grant them access to universities following their completion of the curriculum. While the conclusion of the secondary school platforms will differ based on the institution, the students enrolled in the Lyceum will participate in a mature exam that, if excelled by the student, could grant these students entrance into a university within Poland. Students from these organizations are typically chosen after those from the secondary schools. In 2010, Poland passed legislation that mirrored most of the free world when it banned corporal punishment within the schools. Previously, teachers had been instructed to not enact any form of corporal punishment against students, but this prohibition had few ramifications if broken. That would change in 2010 when it became illegal to participate in any form of corporal punishment within the school. Today, Poland has taken that legislation to a new form by also banning any corporal punishment at home, joining countries such as the United States in their criminalization of parents using brute force with their children.

Students who fare well throughout their education will have the opportunity to attend one of Poland's five-hundred higher level education institutions. Within the selection of these universities, students are able to choose from attending an accredited institution or attending a university that is more specialized in their content delivery. The majority of universities in Poland focus on technology and its attributes while the lowest percentage of universities are centered on theology and its attributes. When compared with universities from around the world, the educational scene in Poland is well-respected with many of the higher education institutions offering advances in the medical and technical fields.

Within the framework of Poland's infrastructure is an impressive healthcare system that has recently become the center of a spotlight on government-provided healthcare. Citizens who have chosen to participate in the healthcare provided by the government are afforded the opportunity to receive complimentary healthcare services performed in hospitals that are operated by the government. Additionally, healthcare facilities are available across the country where anyone is able to go depending on their fiscal opportunity. It has become commonplace in Poland for every city to host its own hospital with most of these hospitals providing standard treatment for their patients. For patients seeking specialized medical attention, there are adequate facilities located in the major cities of Poland, the highest concentration of medical facilities being found within the capital city of Warsaw. Recalling that Poland's own Marie Curie was the discoverer of radium, Poland has one of the leading cancer research centers in the world: the Sklodowska-Curie Institute of Oncology. This center is solely dedicated to the research and mitigation of cancer, attracting scientists from around the world and largely considered to be in the top tier of cancer research centers. Poland's healthcare has done a remarkable job giving treatment to its citizens, largely being responsible for the average life expectancy of 78.5 years. Poland's healthcare continues to be a model that several countries around the world follow while also enticing other countries not yet offering government-provided medical assistance to consider this opportunity for their citizens.

Much of Poland's population is centered within the large cities of Poland. This aligns with the economics of Poland, which show a decreasing agricultural industry and an increasing technological or medical role. Warsaw, the nation's capital, has the largest population with over 1.8 million individuals living in the city. After Warsaw, the differential between the next largest city is stark, with Krakow holding 800,000 residents, over 1 million less than Warsaw. Economists point to the economic centrality of Warsaw as the primary influence in this disparity. While Poland's demographics show a country that is in need of immigration, its positions on education and healthcare reform with the economic surplus that the country enjoys offers unique insight for countries considering such a transition.

THE POLITICS OF POLAND

The politics of Poland are dictated as a representative democracy. As a nation, Poland is governed by a head of state, referred to as the president. While the president retains authority as the head of state, the primary body of legislative power is found in the Council of Ministers, a parliamentary-style government whose governance is facilitated by a prime minister. The dichotomy of leadership between the president and the prime minister is a unique environment but certainly not a unique structure. Following the leadership of other countries such as the United States, Polish presidents are afforded the opportunity to construct a cabinet but does this with the guidance of the current prime minister. Following the democratic structure, the Polish president is elected every five years unless an emergency vacancy occurs at which time the parliament will decide whether or not to hold an emergency election or fill the position with a current position within the government. The body of legislative power, the parliament, reflects a democratic structure with four hundred sixty positions open in what they refer to as the Sejm, the lower house that reflects the House of Representatives from the United States. The upper house, or the Senate, is comprised of one hundred positions. To fill the seats within the Sejm, the country follows the proportional representation method, which focuses on the highest average for filling the seat. To fill the seats of the Senate, the country allows for one senator to represent the body of people comprising one of the one hundred constituencies of the country.

The government is united through the National Assembly, the joint efforts of the Sejm and the Senate. While this body forms a unified government, it is only through the occasion of three different times when the body is fully unified. These times are when the president is the subject of an indictment from the State Tribunal, when the president is elected to his position, or when the seat of president is occupied by someone who is no longer able to serve in the full capacity of his seat. Obviously, with requirements as such, the unification of the government under one roof is a rare experience, at minimum occurring only once every five years. While the legislative branch is considered the most powerful branch of the government, the day-to-day lives of the Polish citizens are governed by the judicial branch of the government. Within the judicial branch, offices such as the Supreme Court, the Constitutional Tribune, the State Tribune, and the Supreme Administrative Court aid the daily lives of the Polish citizens. As a mediator for the Polish people as their representative to the higher courts, the Commissioner for Civil Rights Protection is elected to a five-year term but is not elected via public vote. Rather, the Sejm submits the name of their candidate to the Senate, who then has to approve the figure before they are allowed to occupy that seat. The office of Commissioner for Civil Rights Protection is very important to the lives and freedoms of the Polish people since this position acts as the greatest oversight of new government legislation.

As a governing body, the judicial courts maintain the safety of the lives of the Polish people on a day-to-day basis. The standard by which they derive this safety comes from the Constitution of Poland, which is a collection of principles that are supported by Poland's Civil Law code. Poland was one of the first countries in Europe to demonstrate a constitution, of which multiple revisions took place until an entirely new constitution was adopted in April of 1997. The basic principles outlined in the constitution resembled most democracies, with the citizens of Poland entitled to the rights of free speech, choice of religion, choice of assembly and protest, protections from any medical experimentation, multiple political party affiliations, freedom to assemble a labor union, and freedom from corporal punishment. To ensure these laws are carried out to the fullest extent of the law and to every applicable party, the judiciary branch has implemented a four-tier government system that is comprised of multiple levels of courts, the jurisdiction and power of each court rising from the increasing levels. The most common position within the judiciary branch is the judges, which are given their position for the span of their life. These judges are elected similar to the process of the Commissioner for Civil Rights Protection except that the two parties in this case are the National Council of the Judiciary, the body tasked with submitting nominated judges, and the president, who receives the nominations and appoints the judges if approved. The most powerful positions within the state are occupied by the Constitutional and State Tribunals, respectively. These positions are tasked solely with ensuring that the duties of the statutory law are carried out appropriately. With the statutory law stemming from the positions of the constitution, these two bodies of governance are extremely important to the protected freedoms of the Polish residents.

Within Poland's political structure is the free choice of governing bodies, the Polish residents holding the power to elect anyone to the office of president every five years. The right to vote is held by both men and women, with Poland joining the eleven existing countries in 1918 who allowed women to vote. The safety of Poland is one aspect that has also achieved global attention. Whereas abortion has become a highlighted topic in many countries, Poland has maintained the illegal nature of abortion in all circumstances unless the life of the mother is considered at risk. The only other time when an abortion is allowed is when the fetus is tremendously malformed. Even then, abortions are seen as a tragedy in Poland and are avoided at almost all costs. In additional topics that center on the ethical approach of Poland, the country has also taken a stand for marriage as defined as being between one man and one woman. While Poland may define marriage as such, it has not discriminated against those who defend or identify as a homosexual. Dating back to 1932, homosexuality has been legalized in the country and continues to be practiced by a small group of people in the country.

Within Poland, the country has been divided into smaller divisions known as provinces or "voivodeships" locally. The distribution of land among these various provinces is relatively equal; however, there are a couple of locations that are small as 3,900 square miles, while some can grow as big as 14,000 square miles. Following the example of other countries, the governance of all of these provinces falls on the governors of each province. Additionally, there is an accompanying legislative body within every province that helps spread the judicial branch of the government throughout each province. Just as states in the United States are further extrapolated to find counties, the Polish provinces have been divided further to smaller bodies of land known as powiats. From here, the typical structure of city exists although Poland refers to these bodies of land as gminas. It is not uncommon for some of the larger gminas to also be respected as powiats. In all, Poland has fourteen provinces that help facilitate the country's economy and political structure.

One element of Poland that has been decimated yet returned stronger is Poland's military. Poland's army was at its peak when Poland and Lithuania were united, creating a gigantic army that likely would have ruled Central Europe forever had the partitions never taken place. After the partitions, the Polish Army was grossly unprepared for the future invasion that would come during both world wars. After World War II, the country's military underwent tremendous restructuring until finally beginning to gather its former glory during the early 1980s. Today, Poland's army has subdivided into five distinct branches: the Navy, the Territorial Defense Force, the Land Forces, the Special Forces, and the Air Force. The division of the army as a whole was as recent as 2016 when the special Territorial Defense Force was created. The Territorial Defense Force is Poland's mobile war force, consisting of fifty-three thousand individuals ready to report for battle in less than one day should the country's current military resources be exhausted. The head of the military is the Minister for National Defense, and the President of Poland is tasked with heading up the military for wartime efforts. Prior to mobilizing the Territorial Defense Force, the military capacity of Poland stands at around one hundred thousand troops. These troops are spread evenly among the different branches of the armed forces, the Navy consisting of the smallest group of troops. This is primarily due to Poland's only need for naval resources centering on the Baltic Sea, a rather small portion of Poland's perimeter. In recent times, the Polish Navy primarily trains for search and rescue missions within the sea. In addition, the Polish Navy has also recently become more closely aligned with science, adding a division of the Navy that solely studies the weather and other metrics of hydrography. While the Polish Navy has had little conflict since World War II, it has aligned itself as a close ally of the United States Army, allowing the United States Navy to utilize the intelligence of its Navy while also giving use of measurement software and satellites that were vital in the United States' invasion of Iraq in 2003.

As a member of NATO, Poland's Army primarily maintains the borders of its country, facing very little resistance or attempts at invasion. For a brief period in the early 2000s, the Polish Army maintained a mandatory services in the armed forces for all eligible men in Poland; however, these practices have since been disbanded and the government now focuses on contracting much of its military efforts to agencies within the country. In addition to maintaining the border of Poland, the country routinely sends its resources on peacekeeping missions as outlined by NATO. The armed forces division of Poland's military was an active participant in 2003 when the United States invaded Iraq, aligning two-thousand five hundred soldiers and other resources with the seventeen countries that formed an alliance when invading Iraq. In 2010, Poland's military faced tragedy when the Chief of Army's General Staff was involved in a fatal plane crash. Among those killed was the Commanding General of the Polish Air Force. Poland would weather the tragedy and was able to maintain its strategic positioning despite the loss of leadership.

Poland's military services have long been antiquated, but current efforts are focused on rejuvenating these antiquated practices. In an effort that is set to spend over $35 billion, the Polish military is updating much of its infrastructure and equipment, further positioning it as a formidable force within Central Europe. The pinnacle of the updates includes a new selection of surface to air missiles and updated personnel carriers. With such additions, Poland appears to be well-fortified against the threat of invasion from any side.

While Poland's military protects the citizens from outside threats, the law enforcement of Poland is focused daily on keeping its citizens safe from the threats that pop up within the country. Poland's police force differs little from other countries, with a robust state police system centered on the full-time investigation of crimes while the local police focuses more on the daily protection and service of Polish citizens. Though not used as much, the Polish Border Guard actively protests against illegal immigration into the country. Just as the military of Poland is partially comprised of privately contracted agencies, the Polish police force is aided by the presence of private security firms that manage more mundane security work. To better serve the country's citizens, the country has also established the State Fire Service, which helps protect the citizens from various fire threats while also being on standby for essential emergency personnel. While the State Fire Service is operated by the government just as other countries, Poland has taken their emergency personnel a step further in a manner that distances themselves from other countries. Rather than allow the emergency medical service sector to be managed by private businesses or hospitals, the emergency medical services of Poland are directly operated by the government. This allows the Polish residents to receive complimentary medical services such as ambulance rides and emergency medical responses. As a whole, the country of Poland has taken the protection of its citizens beyond the common measures adopted by other countries.

While Poland has taken special care to maintain the health of its citizens, it has also established itself as a country always willing to help countries in need of services. To facilitate better trade with its neighboring countries, Poland is a full member of the European Union and is an active seat within the European Parliament. In all, an average of fifty seats are always occupied by the Polish government within this parliamentary body. With an aim for peace among all countries, Poland has been an active facilitator of meetings within its own country, absorbing the cost and allowing regional nations to hold peace-seeking talks within Polish government buildings. Poland has been recognized in being perhaps the most powerful country in Central Europe and one that is a key negotiator between countries. Poland's affinity with maintaining its numerous diplomatic relationships has led to its status as the greatest economy within the collection of the Three Seas Initiative. Due to its strategic location and the willingness of the Polish government to help, the United Nations has established the prominent border security office for Central Europe, Frontex, in Warsaw. In addition to maintaining its active membership within the United Nations and the European Union, Poland has also achieved status within NATO and the World Trade Organization, two alliances committed to reducing the barriers of free trade around the world. In a move that many economists attributed to the country's rise from political destruction, Poland has also joined the Organization for Economic Co-Operation and Development, also known as OECD. In an alliance that seeks to align all trade within Europe, Poland is also a member of the European Economic Area, an agreement that allows the member country's citizens the freedom to travel from country to country without the identification normally needed to leave the country. Additionally, this organization has also led to various tax breaks for the citizens as the people are permitted to sell and manufacture goods in various countries without paying excessive taxes.

Even as a country whose infrastructure is leading Central Europe, Poland remains committed to the scientific development within the world, achieving this global initiative by joining various scientific agencies such as the International Energy Agency and the International Atomic Energy Agency. Poland is also a voice of freedom atop the Council of Europe and the Organization for Security and Co-Operation in Europe. Due to the youth of Poland's economic prowess, the country has not been internationally recognized as an economic leader. Its economic success has led to the spotlight of Central Europe, but many international economic boards have long refrained from inviting Poland to occupy a formal seat. There are winds that signify this is changing, however. Recently, Poland was invited to occupy a guest seat at the G20 Summit where the country was highlighted as one of the developing economies in the world. Even though it has not achieved G20 status yet, many economic agencies and even countries have noted that Poland appears to be mature enough to sit on the Summit.

A conversation about Poland's politics is not complete without paying due homage to the country's deepening ties with the United States of America. Poland has always held great respect for the United States, and recent times have shown how far the country is willing to go to maintain this allegiance. The admiration of the Polish government was best seen in 2003 when the Polish government willingly gave access to key intelligence committees to the United States as the War Against Terror campaign kicked off. When the war reached the point of an actual invasion, Poland was among the first nations to give resources to the American government, going as far as to allocate nearly two-thousand five hundred troops to serve on the front lines of the campaign. After pledging the support of these troops to the United States, the Polish government inspired actions from the Australian government, who also sent troops to join the fight. Even as the war in Iraq reaches new phases that do not require the activity of the Polish government, the Polish government has turned its aim to negotiations and mediations. The most recent demonstrations of this came during the administration of President Donald Trump. During key negotiations, the dialogue between the Trump administration and key powers within the European nations has fallen apart. In many of these situations, Poland has rushed to the Trump administration's aid, helping to restart these negations, and in many cases, acting as an influence for the United States' favor. Today, Poland stands tall as one of the leading allies that the United States holds in Europe. Many have pointed to the war in Iraq as taking longer or even facing different outcomes without the aid of the Polish government. Even with the differences of the two countries on various healthcare and social reform measures, Poland's affinity with the United States remains a key relationship that will doubtless show its worth in the future of both countries.

THE GEOGRAPHY OF POLAND

As a nation nestled among a vast array different climates, Poland's weather and geography changes incredibly across the various provinces of the country. From the balmy northwestern coastline of the Baltic Sea to the hot southeastern portion of the country, Poland's climate fits all types. Beginning at the top of the coastline, the country has an admirable coastline that facilitates a good deal of Poland's commerce. Beginning at the western border of the country, the Baltic Sea forms a natural border for much of the northern border, cutting an almost perfect straight line across the top before eventually retreating away from the shoreline.

While the northern border of the country is jutted with a coastline that would resemble that of a lake, it is not solely bordered by the Baltic Sea. There is a remaining portion of the border that is carved out by the Northern European plains. This beautiful country is home to some of Poland's most stunning mountains and basins. In all, there are four major mountain sets that give plenty of breathtaking views of the country. While these mountains take the place of the Baltic Sea for bordering the country, they also have valleys in which are a set of lakes. These lakes are famous for their crystal clear water that will often reflect the beautiful surrounding mountain systems at sunrise and sunset. Of all of these mountain regions, the most famous mountain system is formed by the Carpathian Mountains, whose Tara Mountain juts out above the rest. These mountains are found along the southern portion of the state. In all, there are seventy mountains that cut a beautiful natural skyline in Poland. The mountain system of Poland is one that has achieved significant notoriety in Poland. While the Tatras of the Carpathian Mountains are the highest, the second place position belongs to the Beskids, the highest peak of this mountain ranging nearly one mile. While these two mountain systems are known for their height, other mountain ranges in Poland are more suitable for climbing, the most famous of which are the Table Mountains. This mountain system has an impressive structure of rocks that seem to jut out of the hills at various peaks. Numerous national parks team together to give tourists and residents a beautiful set of trails to explore this mountain system. While Poland is not particularly known for its mountains and hills, these high peaks have given Poland a gorgeous backdrop while also providing shelter for some of Poland's earliest residents.

Surrounded by water and a mountain system, not all of Poland is mountainous. The Vistula Delta, Poland's lowest point, is home to the impressive waterways of Poland. Even with this water system, there is a desert region of Poland, known as the Bledow Desert. Within this desert, the ground lacks significant vegetation due to the terrible conditions brought about by the sand. This desert is 12 square miles and is not visited often. Of particular interest, this desert is different from other deserts in that scientists do not classify it as a desert. Whereas other deserts are natural formations due to climates, this desert was the result of the combination of the mismanagement of land and warfare from neighboring countries during the Middle Ages.

Depending on the scientific beliefs of each geologist, the age of the land mass Poland is centered on could date from 60 million years old to 10,000 years old. Regardless of the exact date, the beauty of this country is evident in the numerous layers of rock formations that contain numerous fossils. The ecosystem of Poland is supported by an extensive waterway system that snakes its way across the country. With rivers allowing the connection of cities, commerce is brought to Poland with the Baltic Sea but is distributed throughout the country in part by the numerous rivers. The longest of these rivers is the Vistula, which pushes water throughout the country for 651 miles. This river is supported heavily by a feed of water from the third-longest river in Poland, the Bug. At 531 miles long, the second-longest river in Poland is the Oder, which is found along the western border of the country and is fed by Poland's fourth-longest river, the Warta. The majority of the rivers in Poland snake their way throughout the country before finally emptying their load of water into the Baltic Sea. The rivers that do not feed the waters of the Baltic Sea are responsible for feeding into the Black Sea. Poland's impressive waterways have given beautiful tours of the country while also providing a means of commerce for the locals through both transportation and fishing.

With most of the rivers in Poland have been around for all of the country's existence, they are a primary means of historical record as their existence and use has given historians a common location to measure events in both time and location with other events. In early history, there are records of the Vikings tribes making their way up the river in their intimidating longboats, either on their way to battle or returning from battle. These travels were primarily the result of the former union that Poland held with Lithuania, a time when Poland controlled most of Central Europe's resources. Even as Poland's waterways have provided the country with fantastic trade and transportation opportunities, the country is also able to maintain opportunities for a clean water supply with many of the springs that bubble around the country. One of these springs is found in Tomaszow Mazowiecki, where a karst spring has been used for virtually thousands of years. The spring is fed by the Pilica River and is a featured part of the Sulejow Landscape Park. Adding to the fame of the spring, its location and rich mineral content combines to form a beautiful array of red and purple rays that reflect from the surface when touched directly by the sun's rays.

As a country with a relatively small land mass, the high concentration of lakes within Poland has distanced the country from other countries, giving it the rich history of having the second-highest number of lakes in Europe, Finland beating Poland with its network of lakes. In all, the country has nearly ten thousand lakes across the country, all of which are greater than 2.5 acres in size. The existence of these lakes has helped maintain what was once the country's leading industry, agriculture, for centuries. The presence of these lakes offers the farmers the opportunity to cut irrigation patterns around the countryside, making most of the country rich in nutrients and ripe for new vegetation. The largest lake in Poland is Lake Sniardwy, which is responsible for nearly 39 square miles of coverage. Its immense size is followed by Lake Drawsko, Lake Lebsko, and Lake Mamry. While the river system of Poland allows the naval transportation between the various provinces like a connected roadway of water, the fishing industry is almost entirely supported by the combined efforts of the Baltic Sea and the lakes of Poland. Not all of Poland's lakes are found on the plains of Poland, however; there is also an extensive array of mountain lakes that dot up in the thousands of miles that are covered by mountains in Poland. Most of these lakes are found in Masuria, also the home to Lake Mary and Lake Sniardwy. The deepest of these mountain lakes Lake Hancza, a member of the Wigry Lake District of the Podlaskie Voivodeship.

Poland's extensive array of lakes offered settlers in Poland the opportunity to live near their chief mode of transportation and food. The historical remains of these villages are still able to be seen in many of the UNESCO sites located around the country. One of these sites is found in the Greater Polish Lake District which is home to the Lusation people of Biskupin. It was here that the earliest residents built stilt houses to protect them from the annual flooding of the rivers and lakes. To protect from the threat of invading forces, numerous castles were also built along the shorelines of these lakes. Today, towers such as the Kruszwica Tower still stand tall along the Lake Goplo, telling the story of heroic Polish people from thousands of years ago.

Today, the Polish waterways are the prime location for the water sports that dominate the springs and summers of Poland; however, the greatest land in Poland is found atop the fertile fields of the agricultural plains in the country. It is difficult for many farmers to find adequate land to farm on due to the extensive forest system that dominates Poland's skyline. With a forest system claiming almost 30% of Poland's land mass, there is a great ecosystem for animals of the forest while also providing ample resources such as timber and firewood. Even with this large forest, the Polish government continues to seek more forestation within the country, attempting to increase the percentage of land covered by forest to 33% in the next 30 years. Despite the extensive forestation, Polish agriculture continues to dominate the country, with most of Central Europe leaning heavily on the agricultural growth of Poland. Today, Poland leads Central Europe in the exports of potatoes and rye. While the agricultural industry of Poland has fallen from its pedestal atop most successful industries, the country continues to provide ample resources for the farming industry to be attractive. As such, the country has nearly 2 million private farms that combine for the agricultural success of the country. In addition to the tremendous grains that are able to be grown on the fertile land of the country, Poland also grows several variants of meat, such as pork, beef, and chicken. Of these three meats, Poland's chief export is pork, further cementing its importance in export to the European Union.

Poland's climate settles on temperate for the majority of the country. While there is a range of difference in temperature from the northern tip of the country to the southern border, the country's average temperate of most of the cities settles around 78' in the summer and 29' in the winter. With the ocean bordering the northern border of the country, the country does not boast the high temperatures usually accompanying a coastline. The higher temperatures are found in the Lower Silesia portion of the country, the average temperate ranging as high as 90' in the summer. Winters in Poland can be brutally cold, dropping as low as 21' in northern portions of the country. However, with temperatures rarely going below freezing, this has created a great climate for the animals of the country, giving the forests a vast array of animals who make Poland their home year-round. Throughout the country, it is not uncommon to see animals such as beaver, moose, deer, wild boar, and even the lynx. With many animals able to be eaten, Poland's forests provide the country with an additional resource that is also favorable to the competitive hunting industry of Poland. Of particular interest to the country,

Poland is known for its strategic location in bird season, giving birds a location to rest due to its temperate climate. The most prominent bird in Poland is the White Stork, which brings 40,000 breeding pairs to the country year-round. Poland's climate has given the country yet another beautiful site, the unencumbered daily lives of animals all available for observation from either the mountains, rivers, or plains of Poland.

CONCLUSION

When looking back on the extensive history of Poland, it is impossible to witness the greatest moments of Poland without also seeing the time periods of tremendous tragedy. When over 50% of a population is destroyed due to the hateful lust of one man, it seems nearly impossible for the country to return to its former glory. And truthfully, Poland did not return to its former glory: it exceeded it. The country went from being demoralized by one of the most tragic concentration camps in the world to being one of the leading economic powers of Central Europe, a country whose existence is seemingly required for Europe's success. The drive and determination of the people of Poland is one that can be mirrored by anyone and is a clear example of how to return from tragedy.

Printed in Great Britain
by Amazon